the SENIOR

MOMENTS

{ MEMORY }
WORKOUT

Improve Your Memory & Brain Fitness Before You Forget!

by **Tom Friedman**

STERLING INNOVATION
An imprint of Sterling Publishing Co., Inc.

New York / London
www.sterlingpublishing.com

STERLING, the Sterling logo, STERLING INNOVATION, and the
Sterling Innovation logo are registered trademarks of Sterling Publishing Co., Inc.

2 4 6 8 10 9 7 5 3 1

Published by Sterling Publishing Co., Inc.
387 Park Avenue South, New York, NY 10016
Copyright © 2010 by Tom Friedman

Distributed in Canada by Sterling Publishing
c/o Canadian Manda Group, 165 Dufferin Street
Toronto, Ontario, Canada M6K 3H6
Distributed in the United Kingdom by GMC Distribution Services
Castle Place, 166 High Street, Lewes, East Sussex, England BN7 1XU
Distributed in Australia by Capricorn Link (Australia) Pty. Ltd.
P.O. Box 704, Windsor, NSW 2756, Australia

Sterling ISBN 978-1-4027-7410-2

Interior design by Michael Rogalski

For information about custom editions, special sales, premium and
corporate purchases, please contact Sterling Special Sales Department
at 800-805-5489 or specialsales@sterlingpublishing.com.

{For my family}

TABLE OF CONTENTS

INTRODUCTION

Imagine being able to improve your memory and sharpen your mental faculties in just a few minutes at a time—and smiling while doing it. No more embarrassing senior moments, acute absentmindedness, fuzzy thinking, or head-scratching confusion. Instead, you'll flex your memory muscles whenever you want, and no one will ever be able to kick sand in your synapses again. All because of *The Senior Moments Memory Workout*.

The Workout is designed for all ages, especially yours. Although dictionaries define a "senior moment" as a momentary lapse of memory, especially in older people—hence the "senior"—forgetful folks in their forties and fifties can be just as vexed by senior moments as those over sixty. That's why no matter how old—or young—you are, you can benefit from the dozens of mental exercises contained in this book.

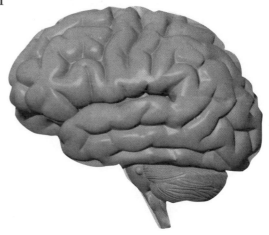

They will engage, intrigue, and amuse you, sharpen your thinking, boost your concentration, and speed up your powers of recall. No heavy lifting. No hidden fees. No special equipment.

Here you will find everything you need to remember how to remember and concentrate on concentrating. There are fascinating quizzes, puzzles, brainteasers, and memory challenges, as well as sound advice and essential information to make you as forgetful-free and clearheaded as possible. Plus there's a sprinkling of historical anecdotes and quotations for reassurance that you're far from alone.

Even the science behind *The Senior Moments Memory Workout* is fresh and compelling. The book's techniques stem from the discovery of "brain plasticity"—the remarkable changes that occur in the brain throughout one's life. Research has shown that experience, knowledge, learning, and recollection can actually alter the way our brains are organized, even in our later years.

For decades, it was thought that the brain inexorably lost nerve cells, or neurons, as we aged, and that we could never grew new ones. But now we know that the brain isn't "hard-wired" as we once believed. It can grow new neurons, tie them together to form new neural pathways, and rewire itself. All we have to do is to keep thinking, learning, experiencing, and remembering—and in the process, "exercising" our brains and memories.

The skills we acquire and the knowledge we gain will all serve to strengthen these new neural pathways, making it easier to access memories of whatever information and abilities we've absorbed. In other words, old dogs *can* learn new tricks.

There is even research suggesting that we can make new "deposits" to our own "cognitive reserve," by keeping our minds active. Simply banking our learning and experience over time may help stave off cognitive problems later.

Now aren't you glad that you finished *A Tale of Two Cities* in school? (Wait—you did, didn't you?) Fortunately, no matter how far behind you've fallen in your reading, it's never too late to contribute to your cognitive account, starting, of course, with *The Senior Moments Memory Workout*.

How should you use the book? Should you begin at the beginning and keep marching through, or can you start anywhere?

Actually, it's completely up to you. Each exercise and piece of advice is independent of all the others. You can go through them in order or skip around. You can do just one exercise when you have a few minutes to spare, or you can keep going. You can spend as little or as much time as you want. This way, you never have to worry about losing your place.

Has there ever been a book about improving your memory and boosting brainpower that requires so little from your memory to begin with? Bring the *Workout* anywhere: to your job, a supermarket, sporting events, parties, the beach, or your favorite restaurant where you can exercise your brain and get useful advice even during your meal—a terrific time saver!

Stumped by a puzzle, quiz, or memory challenge? The answers are in the back, so your stress level never needs to climb too high (an essential feature, since increased stress is bad for your memory).

And if the worst should happen and you lose your *Workout* (which has been known to happen before the full effect kicks in), you only need to buy a replacement. Or two. Or more. Just in case someone "borrows" your copy and forgets to return it.

So let's get started, shall we? One, two, three. One, two, three. And lift. And open. And read!

THE SENIOR MOMENTS MAGIC SQUARE

Since anyone can solve an ordinary Magic Square puzzle (sudoku's proud grandparent), we came up with something special just for you.

In the traditional version of the puzzle, each horizontal, vertical, and diagonal line of numbers must add up to the same sum. Here, however, the definition of "number" has been stretched a bit.

With that in mind, what belongs in the blank squares below, so that the horizontal, vertical, and diagonal lines all to add up to the same amount?

ZERO		0
NOUGHT		VOID
	NADA	

Answers on page 115.

ON BEYOND *ROSEBUD*[1]

If you're old enough to have senior moments, you're probably old enough to remember the following films. Match each movie with its opening line:

1. *Strangers on a Train*

2. *Shane*

3. *Lawrence of Arabia*

4. *To Kill a Mockingbird*

a. "Maycomb was a tired old town, even in 1932 when I first knew it."

b. "He was the most extra-ordinary man I ever knew."

c. "I beg your pardon, but aren't you Guy Haines?"

d. "Somebody's comin', Pa."

[1]*Citizen Kane*

Answers on page 115.

AH, TO BE YOUNGER . . .

It was the year 1201 and a woman in Athens was celebrating her 35th birthday in the warm embrace of her family.

And yet in the year 1206, she had another party to celebrate her *30th* birthday. How could this be?

> { "AFTER THE AGE OF EIGHTY, EVERYTHING REMINDS YOU OF SOMETHING ELSE." }
> —Lowell Thomas

HOME SWEET HOME

Bob leaves home one afternoon as the sun shines brightly overhead. He turns to the right and starts running straight ahead. Then, without stopping, he turns to his left and keeps running, only faster this time. Finally, he turns left once more and picks up even more speed, until he finally reaches home, where he started.

Now that he's back, Bob finds a masked man waiting for him. Who *is* that masked man?

(Hint: No, it isn't Zorro, nor is it the Lone Ranger.)

Answers on page 115.

"REMEMBER ME!"
SAID TOM MEMORABLY

A Tom Swifty is a sentence that ends in an adverb—but not just any adverb. It's one that, while it describes how or when Tom said something, takes the form of a pun.

For example: *"I got first prize!" said Tom winningly.*

A Tom Swifty can also use a more colorful verb to replace the word "said" entirely, as in: *"The optometrist probably doesn't have my eyeglasses yet," Tom speculated.*

Get the idea? Excellent. *"Now it's time to complete the following examples," Tom finished at last.* Good luck!

1. "I have no idea," Tom said _____.

2. "A dog bit me," Tom said _____.

3. "I teach at a college," Tom _____.

4. "I said I wanted a *cold* drink," Tom said _____.

5. "I insist on getting Fido back," Tom said _____.

6. "The judge will find the man guilty," Tom said with _____.

7. "I love the art of Jackson Pollack," Tom said _____.

8. "The hospital can take in more patients," Tom _____.

9. "It's now midnight," Tom _____.

10. "It's not light enough," Tom said _____.

11. "Stop riding that old horse," Tom _____.

12. "The early bird does catch the worm," Tom _____.

13. "It's going to storm," Tom _____.

14. "That's a disgusting joke," Tom _____.

15. "The lemonade needs more sugar," Tom said _____.

In case you were wondering, the name "Tom Swifty" comes from a series of books for boys that was first published in 1910. It featured a young scientist hero named . . . Tom Swift. The original author (in a long line of subsequent writers) was determined to avoid the humble, unadorned verb *said*. And so he wrote the first example of the genre in the very first volume:

"We must hurry," said Tom swiftly.

Answers on page 115.

{ "I'VE A GRAND MEMORY
FOR FORGETTING."
—Robert Louis Stevenson }

BEGINNINGS AND ENDINGS

Try to make two words by using the two pairs of letters you see below, along with six new letters that you must supply yourself.

The first pair of letters, *K* and *K*, forms the middle of the first word.

The second pair, *A* and *T*, forms the middle of the second word.

Now all you have to do is come up with three more new letters that can begin both words and another three letters that can end both.

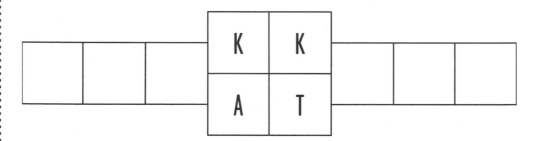

Answers on page 115.

{ "PUT IT OUT OF YOUR MIND.
IN NO TIME, IT WILL BE
A FORGOTTEN MEMORY."
—Samuel Goldwyn }

YOU ARE NOT ALONE
(IN FACT, YOU'RE IN GOOD COMPANY)

British writer G. K. Chesterton frequently forgot to show up for scheduled meetings and then felt obligated to write long letters of apology. He did this so often that his publisher was astonished when the author arrived at the correct time.

Chesterton further surprised his publisher when he handed over a letter explaining why he hadn't been able to keep the appointment.

BRAINY BOTTLENECK

Yes, you *can* try this at home!

If you put a coin in an empty bottle and then plug the bottle with a cork, how can you remove the coin without taking the cork out first?

(Caution: Breaking the bottle in frustration is not an acceptable solution.)

Answers on page 116.

BRAIN is to BODY
as _____[1] is to BOAT

Try to complete the following analogies.

1. BOOT : FOOT as _____ : WHEEL

   a. CAR   **b.** TIRE   **c.** AXLE

2. ORANGE : CITRUS as _____ : GRAIN

   a. CROP   **b.** CEREAL   **c.** WHEAT

3. LAMP : ROOM as _____ : FIELD

   a. SUN   **b.** FLASHLIGHT   **c.** STAR

4. WEB : SPIDER as _____ : WEAVER

   a. WOOL   **b.** HOUSE   **c.** CARPET

5. COWBOY : RANCH as _____ : COURTROOM

   a. JUDGE   **b.** COP   **c.** JURY

[1]CAPTAIN

6. HEAD : CABBAGE as _____ : CORN
   a. HUSKS   **b.** NIBLETS   **c.** EAR

7. CAFFEINE : FATIGUE as _____ : POISON
   a. COFFEE   **b.** ANTIDOTE   **c.** LETHARGY

8. CONFIDENT : ARROGANT as _____ : CHEAP
   a. FOOLHARDY   **b.** RESERVED   **c.** THRIFTY

9. CHANDELIER : CEILING as _____ : ROOF
   a. STALAGMITE   **b.** STALACTITE   **c.** SPELEOTHEM

Answers on page 116.

{ "As I was leaving
this morning, I said to myself,
'The last thing you must do
is forget your speech.'
And sure enough, as I left
the house this morning,
the last thing I did
was forget my speech." }
   —Rowan Atkinson

THE JOYS OF UM-ING AND ER-ING

According to a new study in Scotland, the "ums" and "ers" with which we punctuate conversations can actually improve a listener's ability to remember and understand what's being said.

Researchers asked one group of volunteers to listen to a series of sentences without any stumbles, and then had another group listen to the same sentences with a liberal sprinkling of "ums," "ahs," "uhs," and "ers."

The results? The group that heard the stumbles recalled 62 percent of the information correctly, while the group that got the stumble-free version remembered only 55 percent.

It seems that "disfluencies" such as "um" seem to help the brain pay more attention to what's being said.

Hmm . . .

There is one great danger here. Researchers now want to see if the word "like" can have the same memory-boosting effect. If it does, one can only wonder if the use of the word will spread even, like, further, driving us all, like, insane.

Um, heaven forbid.

A FLAGGING MEMORY

Your visual memory can be just as important as your declarative memory, which handles facts and information.

Anytime you see something, it takes the form of a *mental* image, but this image isn't like a photograph you store in a file cabinet somewhere in your head. Instead, your brain has to *re-create* the original when you try to recall it—unfortunately, with less accuracy as more time goes by.

But the news isn't all bad. If your visual memory is weak, you can strengthen it with practice. For example, look at the four flags below and try to fix them in your "mind's eye." Then turn the page and try to answer the question you find there.

A

B

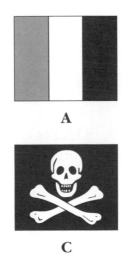

C

D

A FLAGGING MEMORY
(CONTINUED)

So, which flag is pictured below? Is it A, B, C, or D?

Answer on page 116.

{ "MEN FORGET EVERYTHING; WOMEN REMEMBER EVERYTHING. THAT'S WHY MEN NEED INSTANT REPLAYS IN SPORTS. THEY'VE ALREADY FORGOTTEN WHAT HAPPENED." }

—Rita Rudner

THE MONTY HALL BRAINTEASER

Remember *Let's Make a Deal*, the television show hosted by Monty Hall? It appears that playing (and winning) a simplified version of the game has become one of the great brainteasers of all time. It has even fooled some mathematicians.

Here's the setup: Monty shows you three closed doors. There's a car behind one of them, and a goat behind each of the other two. Pick the right door, and you win the car. Pick one of the wrong doors, and you get a goat.

You start by picking a door. (We'll call it Door Number One.) But before you get to see what's behind it, Monty opens one of the two remaining doors (we'll call it Door Number Two) to reveal . . . a goat. Then he asks if you still want to stick to your original choice, or switch to Door Number Three.

What should you do? Open Door Number One as you planned, or change to Door Number Three, which seems awfully inviting now that Monty has planted a seed of doubt in your mind? (Or, if you really like goats, dislike cars, and want to confound Monty, should you instead take the already-opened Door Number Two instead?)

Monty is waiting for your answer . . .

Answer on page 116.

LOST AND FOUND

Sure, you've lost a wallet or purse in your time, but did you ever lose a jackhammer on a bus? Someone in Vancouver did.

The Vancouver transit authority has a veritable museum dedicated to forgetfulness—a museum it quaintly calls the Lost and Found Department.

Only a quarter of all the objects turned in each year are ever claimed. The rest include such seemingly unforgettable items as:

- Artificial limbs
- Oars
- False teeth
- Hard hats
- Full-length mirrors
- Sacks full of cash (my favorite)

In one year alone, the department took in 2,510 cell phones, 3,232 wallets, 2,164 hats, and 440 bicycles.

And the object mislaid far more often than any other, by far? You guessed it: the humble (and all too forgettable) umbrella.

THE CURVE OF FORGETTING

Want to see just how natural forgetfulness is?

Take a look at the *Curve of Forgetting* below. It depicts the speed at which memories fade:

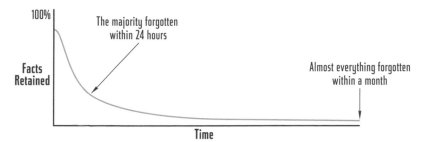

We owe this insight to nineteenth century psychologist Hermann Ebbinghaus, who memorized a list of nonsense syllables and then noted how his ability to recall them declined sharply over time. After nine hours, he had forgotten sixty percent of them. A month later, he had forgotten seventy-five percent.

How can you counteract the decline? One way is to rehearse what you learn until it becomes imprinted in your long-term memory.

Memories of *experiences* also fade over time. When subjects were asked what they did at work the day before, they remembered all sorts of specific events. But when they were asked about the same day a week later, most could only offer a general description.

COMMON WORDS
IN COMMON

What links the following words?

RESTAURANT

ERASER

SORTING

CARRIER

BAKER

CANTERING

LACQUER

RELEASED

ARTIFICIAL

PARTICLE

Answer on page 116.

YOU ARE NOT ALONE
(HONEST)

Legendary actors John Gielgud and Ralph Richardson were performing together on the stage one night when they suddenly stopped.

The prompter, who assumed that one of them had forgotten his line, whispered it quickly. But the two actors remained silent.

Again, the prompter whispered the line. Again, they said nothing.

The prompter, now desperate, called out the line for a third time. Finally, Richardson whispered back, "We know the line, man! We just can't remember who says it!"

{ "IN BOXING, YOU HAVE TO PREPARE FOR MEMORY LOSS. I JUST WANTED TO MAKE SURE I DIDN'T FORGET ANYBODY'S NAME."
—George Foreman,
on why he named each of his five sons "George" }

KEEP TALKING

Isn't it great when something you would do naturally turns out to be especially beneficial?

A new research study suggests that merely talking to another person—a friend, family member, or neighbor for instance—for as little as ten minutes, either on the telephone or in person, can actually improve your memory and boost your performance on tests of cognitive skills.

The psychologist who led the study claims that socializing can be just as effective as more traditional kinds of mental activities in boosting your intellectual performance and memory. The more social interaction, the better the cognitive functioning.

This phenomenon seems to hold true for all age groups. In another study—this one of 16,000 people with an average age of sixty-five—those who were most socially active had the least amount of age-related memory loss.

So what are you waiting for? Get out there and start chatting.

THINK INSIDE THE BOX

What common word or phrase is depicted below?

give   get
give   get
give   get
give   get

COLOR THIS PUZZLE

Ms. Gray, Ms. White, and Ms. Green were having lunch one day when Ms. Gray looked around at her friends and said, "Do you realize that we're all wearing different clothes, and yet none of us is wearing the same color as our own name?"

"You know, you're right," said the woman who was wearing white.

Can you name the color of each woman's clothes?

Answers on pages 116 and 117.

BLESSED ARE THE FORGETFUL

It may seem like a paradox, but forgetting is an important part of remembering. Your ability to block certain unimportant memories enables you to remember what's important, by reducing the demands on your brain.

In one recent study, people who were able to tune out irrelevant words in a word memorization test were able to recall the *relevant* words more accurately. As one report put it, "The brain plays favorites with memories, snubbing some to better capture others."[1]

What is it like to remember almost everything? Scientists studying people with super-memories say that their ability often develops at the expense of emotional intelligence and abstract thinking.

In her memoir, *The Woman Who Can't Forget*, Jill Price explains that her near-perfect memory is more a curse than a blessing. Her memories are so vivid and complete that "It is as though I'm actually living through them again." Worst of all, they force her to relive every sad, humiliating, and painful experience from her childhood, keeping her chained to the past.

"It's hard to grow up," she says, "when you are walking beside yourself."

[1]"Forgetting May Be Part of the Process of Remembering" by Benedict Carey *New York Times* June 2007

BRAIN POWER PUSH-UPS

First, read the paragraphs below (with a straight face, please). Then turn the page and test your memory by trying to answer three simple questions.

Michael and Margaret were so plagued by senior moments that Michael put his wallet in the washing machine and his socks in his back pocket, while Margaret called the dentist to order concert tickets for themselves and their next-door neighbors, Fred and Candace, who had a hamster named Cal.

Concerned, they made an appointment with Dr. Sherman Taft. He explained that absentmindedness typically occurs when your mind is, well, absent. In other words, you can't remember what your memory never absorbed in the first place. This typically occurs when you're engaged in another activity at the same time, such as doing the laundry, calling a dentist, or petting a hamster.

BRAIN POWER PUSH-UPS
(CONTINUED)

Based on what you remember from the previous page, can you answer the following questions?

1. Where did Michael put his wallet?
   a. Outside a country-and-western bar
   b. In the washing machine
   c. Next to the cappuccino machine
   d. At the dentist's office

2. Who is Candace?
   a. The hamster
   b. The dentist
   c. Michael and Margaret's neighbor
   d. The dentist's neighbor

3. Whom did Michael and Margaret consult with?
   a. Dr. Sherman
   b. Dr. Taft
   c. General Sherman
   d. President Taft

Answers on page 117.

WHERE WERE YOU IN THE FIFTIES?

In front of your TV, no doubt, like the rest of us. It shouldn't be hard, then, to match each television series listed below with the family name associated with it:

1. *Lassie*

2. *Father Knows Best*

3. *The Phil Silvers Show*

4. *The Honeymooners*

5. *I Love Lucy*

a. The Ricardos

b. The Kramdens

c. The Andersons

d. The Millers

e. The Bilko

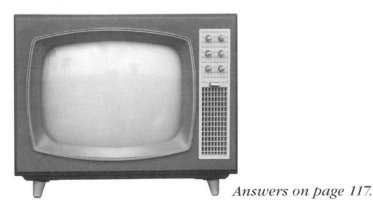

Answers on page 117.

SALMON & EGGS, HOLD THE BACON

No good brain fitness and memory workout would be complete without "brain healthy" foods. Blueberries, for example, contain antioxidants that may help boost cognition. Greek yogurt (the creamy, fattening kind) contains *tyrosine*, which can improve mental alertness.

And don't forget oily fish like wild Alaskan salmon, mackerel, sardines, and tuna, which have lots of omega-3 fatty acids that can promote the growth of neurons needed for the formation of new memories. (A word to the wise consumer: Servings of fish work better than fish oil supplements.)

Then there's the brain-boosting power of eggs. They contain *choline*, necessary for the production of acetylcholine, which also plays an essential role in memory.

So you might want to put salmon and eggs with a side of blueberries and yogurt on your breakfast menu tomorrow morning. But then don't forget to also run around the block 15 times to take off all that extra weight.

BRAINY WORD SEARCH

Find the following words among the letters below. (Hint: The hidden words can run diagonally or even backwards.)

**AMYGDALA   CEREBELLUM   CEREBRUM   CORTEX
HIPPOCAMPUS   NEURON   SYNAPSE**

O	D	U	M	C	E	M	S	P	U	H	C
E	R	M	E	A	U	Y	Y	L	G	R	N
M	M	A	O	S	N	U	E	H	E	R	D
S	U	P	M	A	C	O	P	P	I	H	O
R	L	R	P	Y	U	H	X	C	N	H	R
N	L	S	B	D	G	Y	L	P	R	G	O
E	E	E	E	C	D	S	S	R	C	R
M	B	U	P	O	R	R	A	M	S	N	M
M	E	R	R	G	M	E	M	L	C	B	S
M	R	T	U	O	X	B	C	P	A	B	R
S	E	O	L	A	N	R	E	E	L	O	S
X	C	Y	R	E	U	R	R	A	S	N	R

Answers on page 117.

JUMP ON YOUR HOBBYHORSE

If you don't have a hobby yet, you might want to consider getting one. Research shows that a hobby can:

- Stimulate your thinking
- Sharpen your focus
- Improve your memory
- Help you forget your problems
- Reduce stress
- Increase your energy
- Boost your creativity
- Bring more variety to your life

According to a Harris Poll, the most popular hobbies are reading, watching TV (that's a hobby?), spending time with family members (wait, do they know they're a hobby, too?), gardening, and playing sports. Other polls list surfing the Web, listening to music, playing an instrument, exercising, cooking, doing arts and crafts, traveling, and collecting almost anything as the most popular hobbies.

Since there are countless books, magazines, organizations, websites, and television shows dedicated to hobbies, why not start browsing now?

REMEMBER WHO CAME TO DINNER?

Take a good look at the names of the guests who are sitting around the dining room table. When you think you have a good idea of just who has come to dinner and where they are seated, turn the page.

REMEMBER WHO CAME TO DINNER? (CONTINUED)

See how many names of the guests you can remember, and where they are seated. After you finish, you can always go back to the previous page to see how well you did.

MEMORY JOGGING

Many experts believe that an important weapon in the fight against senior moments is physical exercise. In fact, a major study has found that seniors who have exercised all their lives have significantly better cognitive skills than seniors who were sedentary.

But take heart, all you couch potatoes! It's not too late. Just thirty minutes of brisk walking three or four times a week can actually improve your mental functioning. That's because exercise increases the number of capillaries in the brain, which improves blood flow, which in turn provides neurons with more energy to grow.

The brain uses an astonishing twenty percent of the body's entire blood supply. That constant flow of blood is essential to meeting the heavy energy demands of your neurons.

The brain also requires about twenty percent of the oxygen you breathe. Physical exercise helps to boost your lung capacity so you can take in more oxygen.

Now if only you could remember where you left your sweatpants.

TAKE THAT!
(AND THAT THAT THAT & THAT!)

Try to punctuate the following in order to make it a proper English sentence:

> I said that that that that that man
> wrote should have been underlined.

A BRAINTEASER
THAT SUITS YOU TO A *T*

True or false:

> There are just two *T*'s in the name "Terry Tattle."

(Of course there's a trick. Otherwise it wouldn't be a brainteaser, now would it?)

Answers on page 118.

CHOCOLATE IS YOUR FRIEND—REALLY (SORT OF)

Worried about your memory? In the mood for a snack at the same time? Why not have some chocolate? Or rather, a chocolate-like substance?

Alas, I'm not talking about candy, cake, or cookies but a cocoa-like drink that's made in the laboratory. The drink is concocted from an extract of chocolate that's rich in *flavanols*—a chemical found in cocoa beans—which show real promise for enhancing memory.

Unfortunately, the drink isn't publicly available, at least not yet. But with forgetfulness becoming a major issue as the population ages, there's no telling what entrepreneurs will come up with next. A bar of chocolate truffle flavanols, with or without nuts, perhaps? You can almost hear the announcer now: "Reach for a Flave and remember!"

AT LEAST THERE AREN'T SEVENTY

There are certain things, no matter how unimportant, that you feel you should remember—things that drive you crazy when you can't recall them, especially if you're challenged to do so on the spot.

Such is the case with the names of Snow White's Seven Dwarfs. But fear not. Here's a technique you can use in case of a trivia emergency. Simply remember this mnemonic device (i.e., a short phrase, rhyme, or other mental technique that serves as a memory aid):

Two *D*'s—for Dopey and Doc

Two *S*'s—for Sneezy and Sleepy

Three "feelings"—for Happy, Grumpy, and Bashful

However, if someone asks you next to name all the Muppets, you're on your own.

{ "THE FACE IS FAMILIAR,
BUT I CAN'T REMEMBER MY NAME."
—Robert Benchley }

YESTERDAY, ALL MY MEMORIES SEEMED SO FAR AWAY

Match the following people who've been called the "fifth Beatle" with their actual positions:

1. Derek Taylor

2. Neil Aspinall

3. Brian Epstein

4. D'Artagnan

a. Personal assistant

b. Valiant musketeer

c. Longtime press agent

d. First manager

Answers on page 118.

Answers on page 118.

{ "I HAVE SHORT-TERM MEMORY LOSS, THOUGH I LIKE TO THINK OF IT AS PRESIDENTIAL ELIGIBILITY." }

—Paula Poundstone

WHATCHAMACALLITS

The word "whatchamacallit" (or "thingamabob," "doodad," "whatsit," or "thingamajig"—take your pick) is an incredibly useful way to signal that you don't know, or can't remember, the right term to use. Although I can't help you with "whatshisname" or "whatshername," I can provide you with the correct names of some of those small, seemingly insignificant things you often encounter.

Here are two of my favorites:

1. Once again, you've broken one of your eyeglass "thingies"— that part that goes over your ear—and now you have to get it fixed. If only you could put a name to it. Well, you've come to the right place. That "thingy" is called a "temple."

2. Your hands are numb as you go to zip up your jacket, so when you put the "you know—that thing" into the "doohickey," in order for the "you know—that thing" to fit into "that other blasted thing," your fingers slip. And then, when you pull on the "whatsitcalled" to zip yourself up, the two halves of the zipper separate. Arrgh! If only you could explain what happened without resorting to made-up words or cursing. Well, congratulations! Now you can.

When you put the "pin" at the bottom end of one half of the zipper into the "slider," the pin was supposed to fit into the "box" at the bottom end of the other half of the zipper. But as your fingers slipped, you pulled up the "pull tab" that's attached to the slider to zip up your coat, and in the process, the two halves of the zipper separated. Arrgh!

DOUBLE OR NOTHING

Want to build up your powers of concentration? Pick a small number and start doubling it in your mind. See how far you get.

I'll start you off with the number 2:

2, 4, 8, 16, 32, 64, 128, 256, 512, 1,024, 2,048 . . .

Now try to get up to the fifteenth doubling of 2. How about the twentieth? (You can check in the answer section on page 108 to see if you are right.)

Then, see how far you can get with other numbers, like 3 and 4, without staring off into space and completely forgetting what you are doing, that is.

Answers on page 118.

MICHAEL, ROW YOUR BOAT ASHORE, HALLELUJAH!

Remember being confounded by those brain-crunching logic problems you got in school? Well, now you can redeem yourself by solving this brainteaser.

Michael and his twin children, Jim and Jane, need to cross the River Jordan in their old, leaky boat. But the boat can't hold more than 200 pounds without sinking, and together the three of them weigh 380 pounds. (Michael weighs 180 pounds, and Jim and Jane weigh 100 pounds each.)

How can all three get to the other side?

Answers on page 118.

> "THERE ARE THREE
> EFFECTS OF ACID [LSD]:
> ENHANCED LONG-TERM MEMORY,
> DECREASED SHORT-TERM MEMORY,
> AND I FORGET THE THIRD."
> —Timothy Leary

ALL CREATURES RECALL ODD STORIES TOLD IN CONFIDENCE

An effective way to remember information is to use an acrostic. The simplest kind is a sentence you make by taking the first letter of each word you want to remember, and then using that letter to begin a new word until an entire sentence is formed.

Remember when you learned the nine planets in order from the sun (before Pluto was booted out of the club, that is)? You probably used an acrostic like this one: My (Mercury) Very (Venus) Educated (Earth) Mother (Mars) Just (Jupiter) Showed (Saturn) Us (Uranus) Nine (Neptune) Planets (Pluto).

Now you can use an acrostic in your fight against senior moments. For example, when you need to figure out for the umpteenth time where you left your keys, why not just mutter, "Corey took ballroom dancing before Jonathan did."

Huh, you say? Take another look:

Corey (counter) took (table) ballroom (bed) dancing (desk) before (bag) Jonathan (jacket) did (dresser).

Now try it yourself with your own acrostic.

PUMPING NEURONS

Memories are made by changes in the connections among neurons in the brain. Wonder how many neurons you have? A million? A billion? Actually, it's 100 billion, the number of stars in the galaxy, except they're in an organ weighing just three pounds. (On the other hand, even that many neurons may not seem like enough if you're having a bad day.)

Neurons can respond to stimuli and communicate with each other and other types of cells. They can transmit impulses at a speed of anywhere from 1 to 120 meters per second (about 268 miles per hour).

How do they do it? Simply put (and we mean *really* simply put), it's done with electrical signals and complex chemical changes. All your thinking and remembering is based on these processes.

Think about this the next time you hear the classic slogan "Better living through chemistry." It really should be "No living *without* chemistry."

{ "WHENEVER I THINK OF THE PAST, IT BRINGS BACK MEMORIES." }
—Steven Wright

YOU CAN ALMOST HEAR
A PIN DROP

According to a British retail-consulting firm, one in every four adults has stopped using a debit or credit card because of forgetfulness. They just can't remember their personal identification numbers.

In spite of this, there's another piece of news that should cheer you up. More cardholders *under* forty have this problem than those *over* forty.

TRACKING YOUR PROGRESS

You've taken my advice and started a regimen of aerobic exercise. In fact, you're doing so well, you're able to run a 5,000-meter race.

The crowd roars as you overtake the runner in second place. Question: What place are you in now?

Answer on page 118.

WORDS IN HIDING

There's a word hidden in each of the sentences below. To make things a bit easier, we've included hints to narrow down the possibilities. For example, in the sentence "The cast lets the audience in," the hint might be *The King at home*, with the hidden word being *castle*. ("The **cast le**ts the audience in.")

1. I abhor sentimentality and pretense!
   (Hint: Before I lost my kingdom for it)

2. Mary passes a ladle for the pea soup.
   (Hint: It's green as well)

3. He will be walking unless he is riding.
   (Hint: Don't point that at me)

4. The new tank led the squad into battle.
   (Hint: Careful, don't twist it)

5. Gaspar is a fine young man.
   (Hint: He loves it in the springtime)

6. The Chinese cadres sang patriotic songs.
   (Hint: Hurry and get ready)

7. He never estimates if he can be exact.
(Hint: Taller than all the others)

8. He was not able to paint yesterday.
(Hint: Needs to be polished)

9. Don't step in elephant dung!
(Hint: The needles won't hurt)

10. Cash a local check at a local bank.
(Hint: It's heavenly)

11. A smart person doesn't shake rattlesnakes.
(Hint: Pass the salt, please)

12. What will you do if she won't spin chickens?
(Hint: Ouch, that hurt!)

13. The arts are badly funded these days.
(Hint: It's breaking)

14. His fake scar got torn off.
(Hint: At a snail's pace)

15. She sells light lyres on the seashore.
(Hint: Just a bit) Answers on pages 118–119.

MEMORY, MEMORY, EVERYWHERE

Give your brain a workout by memorizing these lines of Coleridge's *The Rime of the Ancient Mariner*:

> Water, water, everywhere,
> And all the boards did shrink;
> Water, water, everywhere,
> Nor any drop to drink.

Read it to yourself until you think you have it. Then put down the book and try to recite it.

Feeling confident? Why not try the first lines of another nautical gem by John Masefield?

> I must go down to the seas again, to the lonely sea and the sky,
> And all I ask is a tall ship and a star to steer her by,
> And the wheel's kick and the wind's song and the white
>   sail's shaking,
> And grey mist on the sea's face and a grey dawn breaking.

Excellent! Now, how about a real challenge? Say, *The Odyssey*—in its entirety?

"YOU WERE THERE"
(WELL, MAYBE NOT *THERE* THERE)
MEMORY QUIZ

Match the events in the left-hand column with the dates in the right-hand one.

1. Berlin wall comes down; East Berlin tourism goes up ever so slightly

a. 1975

2. Bill Gates and Paul Allen begin Microsoft, on their way to first gazillion dollars

b. 1989

3. U.S. invades tiny Caribbean island of Grenada, and miraculously wins

c. 1977

4. Apple introduces first successful mass-produced PC; paper remains calm

d. 1983

Answers on page 119.

MOTHER GOOSE'S REVENGE

Return with us to yesteryear when you first heard the following head-scratching riddle read to you from a book of nursery rhymes:

> As I was going to St. Ives,
> I met a man with seven wives
> And every wife had seven sacks
> And every sack had seven cats
> Every cat had seven kits
> Kits, cats, sacks, wives
> How many were going to St. Ives?

The odds are your parents never knew the answer, and you never asked. But now, at last, you can puzzle out the solution for yourself (and be fully prepared if your grandchildren ask).

So, how many *were* going to St. Ives?

Answer on page 119.

{ "MEMORY IS LIKE A DOG
THAT LIES DOWN
WHERE IT PLEASES." }
—Cees Nooteboom, Dutch author

YOU ARE NOT ALONE
(WE SWEAR)

The great nineteenth century English artist Sir Joshua Reynolds painted some 3,000 portraits in his lifetime. So it seems inevitable that he would suffer a senior moment at least *once* while wielding a brush.

And indeed, at one point Reynolds painted a man wearing a hat on his head—with the identical hat tucked under his arm.

{ "HERE'S A WAY YOU CAN EASILY KILL A GOOD HALF HOUR. 1. PLACE YOUR CAR KEYS IN YOUR RIGHT HAND. 2. WITH YOUR LEFT HAND, CALL A FRIEND AND CONFIRM A LUNCH OR DINNER DATE. 3. HANG UP THE PHONE. 4. NOW LOOK FOR YOUR KEYS." }
—Steve Martin

THE CIRCLE GAME

Can you turn the rows of O's seen below into a circle by moving just two of the O's?

In other words, turn Illustration One:

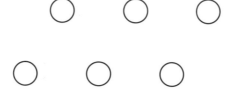

Into Illustration Two:

Answer on page 119.

GOING UP?

Here's the situation:

John lives on the 10th floor of an apartment building. Every morning, he takes the elevator down to the lobby to start his day. Then, when he returns home, he gets back into the elevator to go up to his apartment.

If there's someone else in the elevator, or if it has rained that day, he simply goes up to the 10th floor, just as you'd expect. But if not, he takes the elevator to the 7th floor, instead of the 10th, then gets out and walks up the remaining three flights to his apartment.

Why?

Answer on page 119.

{ "I HAVE
THE WORST MEMORY EVER,
SO NO MATTER WHO COMES
UP TO ME, THEY'RE JUST LIKE,
'I CAN'T BELIEVE YOU
DON'T REMEMBER ME!'
AND I'M LIKE,
'OH, DAD, I'M SORRY!'" }

—Ellen DeGeneres

PLAY IT AGAIN!

Learning how to play a musical instrument is a great way to improve your memory. That's because of all the things you need to remember, such as where to put your mouth and hands and when to tap your foot.

But why stick to the same old choices, like the piano or kazoo, when there are some great alternatives?

Consider the following:

The **bonang** is a Javanese instrument consisting of a double row of bronze kettle gongs mounted horizontally in a wooden frame. It's played with two padded mallets called *tabuh*. (Say, why not get two bonangs and create interlocking melodic patterns using the *imbal-imbalan* technique?)

The **didgeridoo** is a wind instrument that makes a hypnotic, droning sound. Usually around four feet long and made of hollow hardwood, the didgeridoo has been played by the Aboriginal people of northern Australia for at least 1,500 years. (Use it to accompany singers and dancers in traditional religious rituals!)

The **serpent** is a bass wind instrument that's a distant relative of the tuba. It's bent into a snake-like shape (hence the name), has six holes, and was invented in France in the late sixteenth century. Get one and you can finally learn how to play the *Serpent Concerto*—the only serpent concerto, actually—written by British composer Simon Proctor.

If you want to hear what the serpent, didgeridoo, and bonang sound like, check out the website www.oddmusic.com.

If, on the other hand, the piano still calls out to you, but you don't have either the time or money to take private lessons, consider buying an electronic keyboard packaged with special software. It will link to your personal computer, so you can proceed at your own pace whenever you have a spare hour.

And of course there's always the kazoo.

> "'I HAVE DONE THAT,'
> SAYS MY MEMORY.
> 'I CANNOT HAVE DONE THAT,'
> SAYS MY PRIDE,
> AND REMAINS ADAMANT.
> AT LAST—MEMORY YIELDS."
> —Frederick Nietzsche

WHERE *DOES* THAT RAIN IN SPAIN STAY, MAINLY?[1]

Match these great Broadway musicals to their composers and lyricists:

1. *Guys and Dolls*

2. *West Side Story*

3. *My Fair Lady*

4. *The Pajama Game*

5. *The King and I*

a. Leonard Bernstein and Stephen Sondheim

b. Richard Rogers and Oscar Hammerstein II

c. Richard Adler and Jerry Ross

d. Alan Jay Lerner and Frederick Loewe

e. Frank Loesser

[1]In the plain, of course.

Answers on page 120.

FROM LETTERS TO WORDS

Starting with the letters **L** and **E**, add one letter from the group below to form a three-letter word.

D R V I A

You can arrange the three letters in any order you wish. You can pick **A**, for example, to form **ALE**.

Next, select a second letter from the group and add it to the three you already have (again, in any order you wish) to form a four-letter word. And so on and so forth, adding a new letter each time to form a new, longer word, until you've used up all the letters.

Ah, but there's a catch. You must pick the letters in the right order, so that you end with a seven-letter word meaning "matched" or "equaled."

1. _ _ _

2. _ _ _ _

3. _ _ _ _ _

4. _ _ _ _ _ _

5. _ _ _ _ _ _ _

Answers on page 120.

FORGET GINKGO?

The ginkgo biloba tree has been cultivated in China for more than 1,500 years. Today a concentrated extract of its leaves is one of the most popular herbal supplements in the world. Why? Because ginkgo is widely believed to improve memory. But how credible is the claim?

Not very, it seems.

There's little evidence that gingko can actually enhance memory. In a recent study, ninety people ages 65 to 84 and in good health took a ginkgo supplement every day for four months. And yet they performed no better on a series of memory tests than their counterparts in a control group who took a placebo. Other previous studies have reported the same or, at best, inconclusive results.

Ginkgo is now also added to energy drinks, but in such low doses that it couldn't possibly be an active ingredient (except as a marketing tool).

Some side effects of high doses of ginkgo supplements include gastrointestinal distress, nausea, heart palpitations, headaches, and dizziness, so check with your doctor before taking it.

(In more positive news, the ginkgo biloba tree still makes a great bonsai.)

"REALER THAN REAL" IMAGINARY PLACES

Each of the lands below once seemed as real to many of us as our own homes. If only we could have, we might have moved to our favorite one in a heartbeat.

Now it's time to relive your memories by matching the places on the left with the correct city or region on the right:

1. Narnia   a. Eriador

2. Oz   b. Zenda

3. Middle Earth   c. Mildendo

4. Ruritania   d. Cair Paravel

5. Lilliput   e. Quadling

Bonus question: What is the name of the capital city of the lost island of Atlantis?

Answers on page 120.

HONEY, DID YOU SHUT OFF THE OVEN?

According to a survey conducted by a British insurance company, the six most common acts of forgetfulness that result in an insurance claim are:

1. Leaving the house with appliances still running.
2. Failing to check smoke alarm batteries.
3. Leaving the curtains or blinds open, so that burglars can see what's in the house.
4. Leaving for a trip without closing and securing the windows so they can't be opened.
5. Not setting the burglar alarm.
6. Leaving without locking the doors.

Some of these incidents occurred even when people had filed earlier insurance claims for the same memory lapse. Ah well, perhaps they just forgot.

T IS FOR "THINK FAST"

Using the hints below, see how many words beginning with *T* you can remember quickly:

- Spicy sauce (one dash goes a long way)
- Pill (or pad of paper)
- Fishing gear (or football maneuver)
- Large drinking cup (full of ale, no doubt)
- To gossip or reveal secrets (now that's a tale)
- Non-stick coating (dishwasher unsafe)
- Violent storm (see Shakespeare)
- Japanese dish (grilled meat anyone?)
- Christmas decoration (all that glitters)
- Long, furious speech (don't hold back)
- Child learning to walk (first steps are the cutest)
- Native American weapon (can also chop wood)
- You bounced on it (when you were younger)
- Streetcar (Judy Garland sang in one)
- Strolling minstrel (twelfth century romance)
- Flat, treeless area ("Brr . . .")
- The sound of time passing (just ask Grandfather)
- It hides under a bridge (and likes riddles best)
- Pay up now (you're on the road again)
- Whispering party game (Bell's baby)

Answers on page 120.

YOU ARE NOT ALONE (TRUST ME)

When the Nobel Prize-winning chemist Harold Urey ran into a colleague one afternoon, they stopped and chatted for a while.

Then Urey said suddenly, "Say, John, which way was I going?"

The other man pointed the way.

"Good," said Urey. "Then I've had my lunch."

SENIOR MOMENT REBUS

What common word does the picture below depict?

Answer on page 120.

LOCATE YOUR LOCI

Ancient orators first used a memorization technique called the "method of loci" so they could remember their speeches. They imagined themselves walking along a familiar path and associated everything they wanted to remember with the people or things they "saw" along the way.

For example, if your house or apartment is your "path," you might open the front door in your mind's eye and see a small table against the wall, upon which there is . . . ah, yes, that bill you had better remember to pay. Then you might pass . . . hmm, it's your dentist. Aren't you scheduled to see him tomorrow morning, at . . . wait, is that a nine perched upon his head?

You can use the method of loci with any visual image or group of images, as long as they're familiar. One expert memorized the order of ten decks of cards by associating three cards at a time with a mental picture. He imagined the king of hearts, king of spades, and jack of clubs, for example, as Admiral Lord Nelson holding a guitar upside down over a bar in a pub. (Go figure.)

{
"I REMEMBER THINGS
THE WAY THEY SHOULD HAVE BEEN."
—Truman Capote
}

RETURN TO WOODSTOCK
(EVEN IF YOU MISSED IT)

It was such a seminal event in baby boomer culture that at least five million people can recount their memories of the 1969 music festival, even though only one-tenth of that number was actually there.

Of the following performers and groups, which ones were *not* at Yasgur's farm in Bethel, New York, for those three days in August? (Hint: There are four in all.)

Richie Havens
Country Joe & The Fish
Joan Baez
Arlo Guthrie
Joni Mitchell
Janis Joplin

The Who
The Byrds
Jefferson Airplane
Joe Cocker
The Band
Bob Dylan

Sha-Na-Na
The Grateful Dead
Jimi Hendrix
Eric Clapton

Bonus questions:

1. Name the first artist or group to perform.
2. Who wrote the song "Woodstock," which commemorated the festival?
3. Who made it a commercial hit?

Answers on page 120.

TOAST YOUR MEMORY!

Researchers now believe that red wine may help improve your memory. It may also prevent the development of amyloid plaques in the brain, which some believe are a possible cause of cognitive decline in seniors.

The active ingredient in the wine is an organic compound called *resveratrol*. However, resveratrol is only found in red grapes, so you white wine lovers—and beer drinkers, Bloody Mary fans, and Scotch aficionados—are out of luck.

Before you build a wine cellar in your garage, however, there are a few things you should know. You would have to drink a dangerous amount of wine each day to get enough resveratrol to make a real difference, so you might want to wait for a resveratol pill. And although red wine in moderate quantities is thought by some scientists to be good for your general health, excessive drinking can wreck your health. It can cause a deficiency of vitamin B1 (thiamine), which can damage neurons and cause memory loss. As for binge drinking, it can affect memory and cognition for years afterward, even if you stop drinking altogether.

FROM HERE TO THERE

What's the rule that governs the change in the position of both the gray squares and the black squares from Figure A to Figure B?

When you think you have the answer, try to fill in Figure C, on the next page.

FIGURE A   **FIGURE B**

The rule that governs the change from Figure A to Figure B also governs the change from Figure B to Figure C below.

With that in mind, see if you can figure out which of the small squares in Figure C should be gray, which should be black, and which should be left blank?

FIGURE C

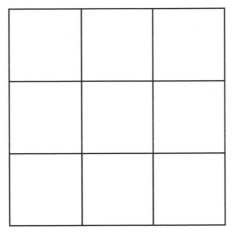

Answer on pages 120-121.

{ "NOTHING IS MORE IMPORTANT
FOR THE 'GOOD OLD DAYS'
THAN A BAD MEMORY." }

—Franklin Pierce Adams

REMEMBER THAT TRIP TO WHEREVER?

Money magazine recently picked the five best places in America to retire—tranquil places where people can learn how to fend off senior moments while hopefully getting a good deal on real estate.

They are: Walla Walla, Washington; St. Simons Island, Georgia; Prescott, Arizona; Holland, Michigan; and Williamsburg, Virginia.

If you were going to visit all five places by car, which of the routes below would be the shortest?

1. St. Simons Island to Williamsburg to Holland to Walla Walla to Prescott

2. Walla Walla to Holland to France to Williamsburg to St. Simons to Prescott

3. Prescott to Walla Walla to Holland to Williamsburg to St. Simon's Island

4. Prescott to St. Simons Island to Williamsburg to Holland to Walla Walla

Answer on page 121.

TAKE A BREAK
(NO, NOT *NOW*—LATER)

If you heard a list of thirty words and then had to recall them, you would probably remember some from the beginning of the list and some from the end, but only a few from the middle. That's how memory works for most people.

But if you take a break, it can reduce this predictable dip in your ability to remember information. Try it the next time you have to fix a large number of facts in your memory and see if it improves your performance.

Studies have shown that splitting up a long session of learning or studying into twenty- to fifty-minute-long periods with five- to ten-minute breaks can give your mind time to relax and stimulate your memory.

So, if you can remember more information by returning to studying with your mind refreshed, why not put down that report or book, or close that laptop, when your mind starts to wander? In other words, just give yourself a break.

JOIN THE GROUP

To absorb a long list of facts or ideas, you can also try grouping together related information. For a demonstration, try to fix these sports in your memory:

Baseball, Skiing, Basketball, Archery,
Soccer, Broad Jump, Football, Wrestling

Not so easy, is it? But what if you took the same list and divided it into two groups—sports that use balls and sports that don't. Then you'd have this:

1. Baseball, Basketball, Soccer, Football
2. Skiing, Archery, Broad Jump, Wrestling

It turns out that we remember information better when it's grouped in a logical way. For example, try taking the place names below and dividing them into two, easier-to-remember groups:

Switzerland, Japan, Syria,
Australia, Mexico, Madagascar

How did you split them up? Did it help? (You can check your groups against mine in the answer section.)

Answers on page 121.

ENDINGS AND BEGINNINGS

Try to make two words by using the pairs of letters you see below along with six new letters you must supply yourself.

The first pair, *N* and *D*, forms the middle of the first word. The second pair, *S* and *T*, forms the middle of the second word.

Now all you have to do is come up with three new letters that can begin both words, and another three that can end both.

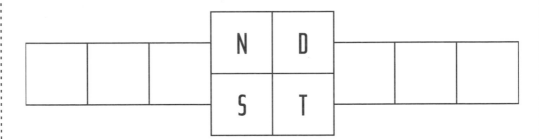

Answer on page 121.

{ "LIKE ALL GREAT TRAVELERS,
I HAVE SEEN MORE THAN I REMEMBER,
AND REMEMBER MORE
THAN I HAVE SEEN." }

—Benjamin Disraeli

FRESHEN YOUR CUP?

Good news for coffee lovers—and Starbucks. Researchers now suggest that coffee may cut the risk of dementia and its attendant memory loss by blocking the damage that cholesterol can cause in our bodies.

According to the *Journal of Neuroinflammation*, a laboratory experiment involving rabbits that were fed a diet rich in fat showed that a vital barrier between the brain and the animal's main blood supply was protected in those given a caffeine supplement. (No word yet on whether a *venti* low-fat cappuccino might have worked even better.)

It turns out that coffee beans are full of antioxidants, which are thought to be good for brain health. In fact, coffee may be one of the top sources of antioxidants in our diet (which just goes to show how much room there is for improvement).

Not a coffee drinker? No problem. Green tea is also being touted as a brain-healthy beverage due to its high level of antioxidants known as *polyphenols*. Researchers have recently suggested that drinking large quantities of green tea may help prevent memory loss in people suffering from sleep apnea, a common sleep disorder.

However, as with all claims, keep an eye out for any new research.

WHO SAID IT?

Who uttered the following immortal words? (So immortal, we're hoping you remember them.)

1. "The secret of staying young is to live honestly, eat slowly, and lie about your age."
   a. Lucille Ball
   b. Doris Day
   c. Debbie Reynolds

2. "Sincerity is the secret of success. If you can fake that, you've got it made."
   a. Woody Allen
   b. Groucho Marx
   c. George Burns

3. "If Lincoln were living today, he would turn over in his grave."
   a. Dan Quayle
   b. George W. Bush
   c. Gerald Ford

4. "We were both in love with him. I fell out of love with him, but he didn't."

    a. Zsa Zsa Gabor

    b. Bette Davis

    d. Cher

5. "Include me out."

    a. Yogi Berra

    b. Sam Goldwyn

    c. Casey Stengel

6. "I do not stand on protocol. If you just call me 'Excellency,' it will be okay."

    a. John C. Danforth

    b. John Kenneth Galbraith

    c. Henry Kissinger

7. "Before I refuse to take your questions, I have an opening statement."

    a. Donald Rumsfeld

    b. Ronald Reagan

    c. Richard Nixon

Answers on page 121.

WHAT, ME WORRY?

You're running late. You have too much to do. You're getting anxious. You're feeling stressed. And you're also becoming more forgetful.

Here's why: Too much stress can trigger the release of a hormone called *cortisol*, which can interfere with memory.

According to the latest research, even a single episode of severe stress can kill off new nerve cells in the brain. (This is why post-traumatic stress disorder, or PTSD, is such a terrible problem for soldiers returning from war, victims of violent crime, and survivors of natural disasters.)

If too much stress is bad for your memory, shouldn't lowering it be helpful? The answer is a definite *yes*.

So here's the question: Of the following "stress reducers," which do you think have been proven to work?

1. Taking a hot bath
2. Allowing 15 extra minutes to get to appointments
3. Saying "no" to activities you don't have time for
4. Taking more breaks during the day
5. Becoming more flexible about what you expect from other people and yourself

6. Talking out a problem with a friend, colleague, or family member

7. Doing just one thing at time (compulsive multitaskers, this is for you)

8. Learning to delegate

9. Taking care of important tasks first

10. Doing a favor for someone else

11. Being prepared to wait if necessary by bringing along a book or an iPod (but *not* extra work)

12. Making time for a daily walk

13. Getting up and stretching

14. Breathing deeply for several minutes

15. Going to a quiet place with no distractions

16. Listening to the sounds of nature

17. Moving to a new town where you don't know a soul, starting a new job, building a new house, running for public office, and raising a bear cub in the kitchen

If you picked any (or all) of the first 16, you're right—and now all you have do to is try them.

If you picked number 17, however, you might want to go on a very long vacation. Tomorrow.

DOUBLE YOUR FUN

Fill in the puzzle grid below using these six pairs of extra letters:

A A   E E   I I   K K   N N   T T

Your challenge is to form four new words, and then use each word twice (eight words in all).

You must use all the letters above and all the letters already in the grid. Furthermore, each horizontal and vertical line of letters must form one of the four words. (And remember, each word must appear twice.)

L			
	D		
		C	
			E

Answers on page 121.

SHIRLEY MACLAINE, TAKE NOTE

Tellingly, people who think they remember their "past lives" may be more likely to make certain types of memory mistakes.

In an experiment conducted in the Netherlands, believers in reincarnation were asked to read aloud from a list of names of people who were unknown to them and not at all famous. After a two-hour wait, they were then given a second list with three types of names; those of famous people, those of non-famous people who were also on the first list, and those of non-famous people who were not on the first list.

The results? Believers in past lives were twice as likely to identify as famous the non-famous people who had been on that previous list. In other words, they couldn't remember where their memories of the names came from. They just assumed that the people must be famous and that they had encountered the names somewhere outside the experiment.

The researchers speculated that believers in reincarnation might find it easier to convince themselves of things that aren't true because they have trouble remembering how and when they learned information. They then convince themselves that they actually *experienced* the events they only heard or read about.

TEN-SECOND DASH

Solve each of the puzzles below by starting on the left with the first number and then working your way across—following the instructions in each box—until you reach the end.

See if you can finish each puzzle in less than ten seconds.

1.

30	÷6	× 4	- 8	÷ 3	× 2	=

2.

23	− 5	÷ 6	+ 4	× 3	− 7	=

3.

12	− 7	× 3	+ 6	÷ 3	+ 4	=

Answers on page 122.

NINE DOTS
TO A SHARPER BRAIN

Starting from one of the dots below, draw four continuous lines without lifting your pencil. The catch? By the end, each dot must have a line running through it.

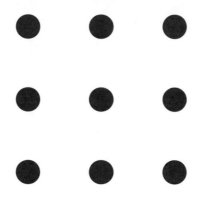

Answer on page 122.

{ "WE FORGET ALL TOO SOON
THE THINGS WE THOUGHT
WE COULD NEVER FORGET."
—Joan Didion }

A HARD WORD TO REMEMBER

Here's an uncommon word (to say the least) that you can drop into conversations with your forgetful and absentminded friends.

It's *athazagoraphobia*, a real but little-known syndrome. First, guess which of the following definitions is the right one:

1. The fear of remembering something that never happened
2. The fear of remembering something that did happen
3. The fear of forgetting or being forgotten
4. The fear of never having existed

If you picked number 3, you're right. But the correct definition is *not* what we're going to ask you about on the next page.

A HARD WORD
TO REMEMBER (CONTINUED)

Which of the following means "the fear of forgetting or being forgotten"? (You know, the word you just learned?)

1. azagoraphobia
2. athagoraphobia
3. athazagoraphobia
4. azathagoraphobia

Answer on page 122.

> "THE GENERAL ROOT
> OF SUPERSTITION
> IS THAT MEN OBSERVE
> WHEN THINGS HIT,
> AND NOT WHEN THEY MISS,
> AND COMMIT TO MEMORY THE ONE,
> AND PASS OVER THE OTHER."
> —Sir Francis Bacon

UNRULY LETTERS

You just can't trust letters to line up in order, especially when you're trying to turn them into words. So sometimes you just have to try harder—with a little extra brainpower.

Unscramble the following words to find the one in each set that goes with the clue.

1. Fragrant flower
   a. stucca
   b. neindl
   c. crihb
   d. clali

2. Unit of volume
   a. lmieorket
   b. trileiliml
   c. matfoh
   d. dupno

3. Mortal enemy
   a. drclaaen
   b. mrreepnfac
   c. esimnse
   d. htpeuck

4. Game of chance
    a. treulote
    b. kycoeh
    c. scarlose
    d. ghupjimh

5. Certain Transylvanian
    a. grapedit
    b. sotorre
    c. previma
    d. hazepicmen

6. Capital on the Mediterranean
    a. ooternp
    b. raglies
    c. dyesny
    d. coupalac

7. Classic novel
    a. ijanodanesin
    b. obruurselb
    c. claftimage
    d. draweapcane

Answers on page 122.

"YOU WERE THERE"
(OR IF NOT THERE, NEARBY)
MEMORY QUIZ

Match the events in the left-hand column with the dates in the right-hand column.

(You were paying attention back then, weren't you?)

1. Watergate forces Nixon's resignation; all future scandals must now end in *-gate*   **a.** 1967

2. First Super Bowl played; first Super Bowl commercials are aired   **b.** 1974

3. Neil Armstrong lands on the moon, but finds no McDonalds or Kentucky Fried Chicken   **c.** 1971

4. Eighteen-year-olds finally get the right to vote, but are otherwise occupied   **d.** 1969

Answers on page 122.

YOU ARE NOT ALONE
(BELIEVE IT)

Actress Joan Collins visited the National Press Club in Washington one day to promote her latest book about how modern society unfairly stereotypes older people.

Unfortunately, just as she was about to tell the audience the title of the book, her mind went blank.

"It's called," she said, struggling mightily to remember. "What *is* it called?" ("The Art of Living Well," actually—but not *too* well, it seems.)

> "WHEN I WAS YOUNGER, I COULD REMEMBER ANYTHING WHETHER IT HAD HAPPENED OR NOT; BUT MY FACULTIES ARE DECAYING NOW AND SOON I SHALL BE SO THAT I CANNOT REMEMBER ANYTHING BUT THE THINGS THAT NEVER HAPPENED."
> —Mark Twain

THE TREASURE OR THE TIGER?

Imagine that you're in a room with two doors. (How you got there in the first place is not important.)

Behind one of the doors is a treasure you can take with you on your way out.

Behind the second door, however, is a ferocious and exceedingly hungry tiger waiting impatiently for lunch.

Unfortunately, you don't know which door is which.

Fortunately, there are two other people in the room who may be able to help. The first is a knight who always tells the truth, while the second is a dastardly thief who always lies.

Unfortunately (there's that word again), you can't tell the two of them apart. (You didn't expect an easy brainteaser, did you?)

Fortunately, you can ask one of them a question. Unfortunately, that's only one question to only one person.

So here's the challenge: what question should you ask to be absolutely certain the door you open has the treasure behind it, and not the tiger?

Answer on page 122.

A RISING TIDE

Picture this scene (unless you're prone to acute seasickness, that is):

There's a boat in the harbor, gently bobbing up and down. Hanging over the side is a rope ladder that barely reaches the surface of the water. The ladder has six rungs, each a foot apart.

Question: How many rungs will be underwater if the tide rises three feet? How many rungs will be underwater if it rises six feet?

CRACK THE CODE

Challenge your brain to a wrestling match by decoding the following:

1. EB REDNEL A RON REWORROB A REHTIEN

2. TIW FO LUOS EHT SI YTIVERB

3. TLEM DLUOW HSELF DILOS OOT OOT SIHT TAHT O

4. EB YAM EW TAHW TON WONK TUB ERA EW TAHW WONK EW

Answers on page 123.

ABOKATU BATEKIN HITZ EGIN NAHI DUT[1]

Experts agree that learning a new language can help strengthen your memory by forcing you to remember a large amount of new information. But which language is right for you?

If you need a major memory boost, how about Basque, spoken in parts of Spain and France? Some experts call it the most difficult language of all to learn. Intrigued? Try this traditional phrase on for size: "Hartzen al duzue kreditu txartelik?"[2]

Or how about the language with the world's largest alphabet—Cambodian—with three times as many letters as English? Or the language of the Ubykh people in the Caucasus, with 82 consonant sounds? (Unfortunately, Tevfik Esenç, the last proficient speaker, died in 1992.)

On the other hand, if you just need a minor memory tune-up, why not try Taki Taki, also known as Sranan, spoken in Suriname in South America? It has a total of 340 words.

---

[1] "I want to talk to a lawyer!" in Basque
[2] "Do you accept credit cards?"

RIDDLE YOU THIS

To those of you who still recall the riddles of your childhood, used as a diabolical form of mental warfare, we apologize for asking you such familiar ones.

On the other hand, to those of you who haven't heard a riddle in years, we apologize if you wind up slapping your forehead in frustration and muttering "Of course!" when you learn the answers.

1. What kind of coat can only be put on when wet?

2. What can you catch but not throw?

3. What is it that, after you take away the whole, some still remains?

4. What can run but never walks, has a mouth but never talks, has a head but never weeps, has a bed but never sleeps?

5. What goes around the world but stays in a corner?

6. "I'm lighter than a feather, but you can't hold me for more than a minute. What am I?"

7. The more you take, the more you leave behind.

8. What goes around the house and in the house, but never touches the house?

9. What can you keep after giving it to someone else?

10. What belongs to you, but other people use it more than you do?

11. What do you break as soon as you name it?

12. What is it that comes with a car, goes with a car, and is of no use to a car, but the car can't go without it?

13. What is put on a table and then cut, but is never eaten?

14. What holds water but is full of holes?

15. When you don't know what it is, it's something, but when you do know, it's nothing.

Answers on page 123.

> "WHY IS IT THAT OUR
> MEMORY IS GOOD ENOUGH TO
> RETAIN THE LEAST TRIVIALITY
> THAT HAPPENS TO US,
> AND YET NOT GOOD ENOUGH
> TO RECOLLECT HOW OFTEN
> WE HAVE TOLD IT
> TO THE SAME PERSON?"
> —François de La Rochefoucauld

POWERS OF RECALL

Perhaps the toughest memory challenge is also the simplest.
See how many of the following questions you can answer
correctly. (You can even count the near misses.)

- What were doing an hour ago?
- What were doing at this time yesterday?
- What were doing a week ago?
- What were you doing a month ago?
- What were you doing a year ago?

SCRABBLE SCRAMBLE

You're playing a cutthroat game of Scrabble with the letters
below, and you need to come up with a seven-letter word in only
seven seconds.

Can you retrieve the word from your memory in the nick
of time?

T F G R S O E

Answer on page 123.

WHY *DID* YOU COME INTO THIS ROOM?

Let's try to jog your memory with some likely reasons. Perhaps you're here to:

- Read this book
- Find your glasses
- Find your keys
- Find your wallet or handbag
- Pay the bills
- Make a phone call

- Search for the TV remote
- Get that thing
- Put back that thing
- Actually, you meant to go into another room entirely

You can try to prevent this kind of memory lapse in the future by saying out loud or visualizing whatever you intend to look for, as soon as you think of it—that is, *before* you enter the room. This way, the information will enter your memory and stay there (at least for a while).

But it's very important not to get sidetracked. So, avoid at all costs any intervening discussions about whose turn it is to walk the dog or take out the garbage.

NAME THAT GURU!

They attracted millions in the '60s and '70s. The Hindu terms *guru* (spiritual teacher) and *ashram* (spiritual retreat) became household words, and "Hare Krishna Hare Krishna" was chanted in airports.

Now it's time to plumb the depths of your cultural memory by matching each guru below with his chief claim to fame in the Western media.

1. Maharishi Mahesh Yogi

2. Swami Prabhupada

3. Swami Satchidananda

4. Bhagwan Shree Rajneesh

a. Deported from the US after pleading guilty to fraud

b. Popularized Transcendental Meditation; attracted stars

c. Founded the Hare Krishna movement

d. Spread the practice of yoga and spoke at Woodstock

Bonus Question: What comes after "Hare Krishna Hare Krishna"?

Answers on page 123.

RACING HORSES, RACING MINDS

A crafty rancher on the verge of retirement asked his son and daughter to race each other on horseback across one hundred miles of the wildest territory in the Southwest.

For years, both siblings had boasted that their horse was faster. So the father announced that the owner of the winning horse would get to manage the patriarch's vast holdings. According to his rules, however, the owner of the *slower* horse, not the faster one, would be the winner, confounding his son and daughter.

And so for days the siblings wandered aimlessly across the forbidding landscape, each afraid to get to the finish line first, since it would mean that their sibling's horse was slower than their horse, and thus the winner.

Finally, in desperation, they asked a Native American elder for advice. After they heard his reply, they raced as fast as they could to the finish line. What did the wise man say?

Answer on page 123.

YOU ARE NOT ALONE
(NOT EVEN REMOTELY)

A sports fan from Boston was about to go back to his hotel in Hanover, Germany, after a World Cup soccer match. He had just checked in that afternoon, but when he left the stadium he realized he had forgotten the hotel's name and address.

For six hours, he wandered the city hoping that something would jog his memory. Finally, he walked into a police station and begged for help. The only thing he could remember was that his taxi ride to the stadium cost ten euros and took him past a park and a Mercedes dealer. This in a city of 500,000.

After the police spent an hour driving him in a "10 euro radius," the fan finally recognized his hotel, much to everyone's relief. (No word on whether he dared to leave his room the following day.)

{ "THERE ARE LOTS OF PEOPLE WHO MISTAKE THEIR IMAGINATION FOR THEIR MEMORY." }
—Josh Billings

A SLICE OF PI WITH A LESSON ON TOP

Travel back with us to that magical time when pi wasn't something you ate, but something you had to remember—preferably, just before a test.

By definition, pi (π) is the ratio of the circumference of a circle to its diameter. You need it to calculate the area of a circle: $\pi \times r^2$ (with *r* being the radius).

You probably used the first three digits of pi: **3.14**. But here is your chance to challenge yourself (and impress all those teachers who rolled their eyes at your ignorance) by memorizing pi to the *seventh* digit—that is, **3.141592**—and in the process, learn an important technique for remembering information.

You're going to be using the technique of "chunking," which breaks up information into more manageable pieces, or "chunks." Trying to remember seven digits won't seem nearly as difficult if you just think about your phone number—which, after all, has seven digits (excluding area code, of course). That's no accident, since our working memory can hold an average of seven bits of information.

So now you can turn **3.141592** (or any other seven digit number, like the account numbers you keep forgetting) into a "phone number" to help you remember it: **314-1592.**

HAVE A BALL!

This should bring you back a few years (or perhaps a few decades).

How can you throw a ball as hard as you can and still have it come back to you—*if*:

1. It doesn't hit anything?
2. There is nothing attached to it?
3. No one catches it and throws it back?

IT MUST HAVE BEEN A VERY, VERY, *VERY* LONG WEEK

TGI Friday!

Oh, wait. Sorry. It's not Friday at all—at least not in this brainteaser.

Name four days that start with the letter *t*.

Answers on page 124.

ALWAYS REMEMBER TO DOT YOUR *i*'S

As you read the paragraph below at your normal speed, try to count all the *i*'s (without using a pencil):

"There was pressure to produce in greater volume in order to get production costs down. According to the so-called 'experience curve,' for every doubling of production volume in manufacturing, the cost per unit drops about twenty percent—as workers become more adept, machines become more efficient, and the manufacturing system is continually improved. In the pocket-calculator market, that meant prices would be coming down fast. It's why prices can come down fast on any new product that achieves sudden popularity— from color TVs to the Rubik's Cube."

Check the answer section to see how many i's there really are. If you missed three or less, go ahead and give yourself a pat on the back. If you caught them all, congratulations. You get to ask someone *else* to pat you on the back. (It's safer that way.)

Answer on page 124.

WHAT COMES NEXT?

Take a look at the three series of four letters below. Every letter in each series is really the first letter of a word, and all the words in a series are related.

For example, if the first four letters of a series were **M, V, E, M,** they would stand for **M**(ercury), **V**(enus), **E**(arth), and **M**(ars).

So logically, the next four letters would be **J** for Jupiter, **S** for Saturn, **U** for Uranus, and **N** for Neptune—the planets in order from the sun.

First, look at each string of letters below to figure out what specific words they stand for.

Then, after you've done that, you should be able to complete each string with four *new* letters, which stand for four new words.

1. **J, D, N, O,** __ __ __ __
2. **T, F, F, S,** __ __ __ __
3. **H, R, T, E,** __ __ __ __

Answers on page 124.

{ "ONE LIVES IN THE HOPE
OF BECOMING A MEMORY."
—Antonio Porchia }

TO SLEEP, PERCHANCE TO REMEMBER

According to the Sleep Council, one out of five people suffer from a lack of sleep, and a common cause of memory loss is chronic fatigue. Ideally, you should be getting from seven to nine hours of sleep each night.

If you can't, a nap can speed up the consolidation of new memories. How long should the nap be? Scientists first said about sixty to ninety minutes, but now some are suggesting that even shorter "power naps" may also help boost your memory.

In one study, college students were given a list of thirty words to study and remember, and then tested an hour later. But it's what happened in between that really counts. One group of students took a 6-minute nap, a second group took a 35-minute nap, and a third group stayed awake.

The results? As expected, taking 35-minute naps produced higher scores on the memory test than staying awake. But surprisingly, taking 6-minute naps also produced higher scores (although not as high as the longer naps).

So stop fooling around and start snoozing!

WORDS, WORDS, WORDS

For each set of three words below, find a fourth word, which, when added to the others, forms a compound word or a word pair.

For example, for a set including *smith*, *fore*, and *game*, the answer would be *word*, as in wordsmith, foreword, and *word game*.

Ready?

1. poke, motion, down
2. wood, luck, times
3. watch, light, sign
4. style, saver, time
5. off, business, case
6. blue, cottage, cake
7. maiden, made, open
8. lunch, top, luxury
9. let, red, hawk
10. chuck, work, hard
11. remover, light, hot

Answers on page 124.

"YOU WERE THERE"
(OR YOU KNOW SOMEONE WHO WAS)
MEMORY QUIZ

Match the events in the left-hand column with the dates in the right-hand column:

1. Alaska and Hawaii became states; US Senate had to find four more chairs

    a. 1957

2. Capitol Records convinced Beatles won't sell in US; executives kept jobs

    b. 1959

3. Sputnik launched; epidemic of stiff necks as human race looked up at night sky

    c. 1962

4. Cuban Missile Crisis erupted; world had anxiety attack

    d. 1963

Answers on page 124.

POPPING PILLS TO
REMEMBER, NOT TO FORGET

One out of five readers of the British science journal *Nature* admitted that they're trying to sharpen their mental performance and memory by taking drugs such as Ritalin, Provigil, and Inderal.

These medications are commonly prescribed for attention-deficit hyperactivity disorder, or ADHD—a condition these readers do *not* have.

Some health professionals fear that these drugs are already over-prescribed for ADHD, let alone for other purposes. But when *Nature* readers were asked how they felt about any professionals using the drugs to enhance their cognitive performance, eighty percent said that it didn't bother them at all and should be allowed. Nearly seventy percent said that they would consider taking the drugs themselves.

What's the real price for taking this kind of shortcut to a better memory? How about side effects including irritability, anxiety, insomnia, reduced appetite, headache, upset stomach, increased blood pressure, and/or depression?

TIPPING THE SCALES OF FORTUNE

Let's say you keep a collection of 23 gold coins in a box on your desk, but by accident you've just put in another coin that's far more valuable than all the rest.

Unfortunately, this rare coin can only be identified by its weight—the result of a mistake at the East Morovian Mint, which added more gold than necessary, thus making it heavier than the other 23.

You now need to find it quickly so you can sell it to a rich and impatient collector. The problem? You're not allowed to identify it by weighing each coin individually, as anyone else would do. (Why? Because it wouldn't be a puzzle otherwise.)

Instead, you must find the one you want by dividing all 24 coins into piles (we're not saying how many piles, naturally), and then weighing two piles at a time on a balance scale.

The good news: To help you with the process of elimination, you can use different piles of any size each time you use the balance scale. (Sorry. That's the only good news.)

How many weigh-ins will it take to find the heavier and much more valuable coin?

Answer on page 124.

AND THE NEXT NUMBER IS...

What number comes next in each sequence?

1. 4, 7, 12, 19, 28, _____
    a. 31
    b. 33
    c. 39

2. 6, 20, 27, 41, 48, _____
    a. 62
    b. 67
    c. 70

3. 23, 16, 10, 5, 1, _____
    a. 0
    b. -1
    c. -2

4. 9, 18, 54, 216, 1,080, _____
    a. 5,420
    b. 6,480
    c. 6,860

Answers on page 125.

YOU ARE NOT ALONE (TRULY)

Even Thomas Edison, the Wizard of Menlo Park, had senior moments. The inventor often found visitors in his office, helping themselves to his Havana cigars. Edison was extremely annoyed, but didn't want to lock up the cigars and then have to waste time retrieving them. So an assistant suggested the following:

What if the assistant's friend who was in the cigar business made some fake cigars out of cabbage leaves? They could then be substituted for the genuine Havanas.

Edison agreed to the plan, but forgot all about it soon after. He only remembered when he came back from a trip and asked his assistant where the bogus cigars were. The assistant explained that they had arrived before Edison left and had been passed on to the lab's manager.

So Edison called the manager, who explained that he had packed them in Edison's bag before the inventor's trip.

"And do you know," Edison recalled later, "I smoked every one of those damned cigars myself!"

{ "CREDITORS HAVE BETTER MEMORIES
THAN DEBTORS."
—Benjamin Franklin }

THE MISSING LINKS

Can you supply what's missing from the following group of letters, and thereby return them to their full glory?

1.   "WHLDTHSTRTHSTBSLF-VDNT, THTLLMNR

CRTDQL, THTTHYRNDWDBTHRCRTR

WTHCRTNNLNBLRGHTS, THTMNGTHSRLF,

LBRTY, NDTHPRSTFHPPNSS. THTTSCRTHS

RGHTS, GVRNMNTSRNSTTTDMNGMN,

DRVNGTHRJSTPWRSFRMTHCNSNTFTH

GVRND, THTWHNVRNYFRMFGVRNMNT

BCMSDSTRCTVTTHSNDS, TSTHRGHTFTH

PPLTLTRRTBLSHT, NDTNSTTTNW

GVRNMNT, LYNGTSFNDTNNSCHPRNCPLS

NDRGNZNGTSPWRSNSCHFRM, STTHMSHLL

SMMSTLKLYTFFCTTHRSFTYNDHPPNSS."

2.	"THWRLDWLLLTTLNT, NRLNGRMMBRWHT
WSYHR, BTTCNNVRFRGTWHTTHYDDHR. TS
FRSTHLVNG, RTHR, TBDDCTDHRTTH
NFNSHDWRKWHCHTHYWHFGHTHRHVTHS
FRSNBLYDVNCD. TSRTHRFRSTBHRDDCTD
TTHGRTTSKRMNNGBFRS—THTFRMTHS
HNRDDDWTKNCRSDDVTNTTHTCSFRWHCH
THYGVTHLSTFLLMSRFDVTN—THTWHR
HGHLYRSLVTHTTHSDDSHLLNTHVDDN
VN—THTTHSNTN, NDRGD, SHLLHVNW
BRTHFFRDM—NDTHTGVRNMNTFTHPPL,
BTHPPL, FRTHPPL, SHLLNTPRSHFRTHRTH."

Answers on pages 125-126.

WHEN YOUR BRAIN TAKES A VACATION

Ever wonder what happens in your brain when you make a mindless mistake?

Researchers have discovered that activity in the frontal lobe of the brain, which controls working memory and cognition, gradually decreases just before a mistake is made. At the same time, activity increases in several other parts of the brain, known collectively as the "Default Mode Network."

These two changes begin as early as thirty seconds *before* an error is made. The changes were revealed by a functional magnetic resonance imaging machine (fMRI), which identified changes in blood flow and oxygenation in the brain. And what were the subjects doing while confined in the imager? They were reacting to the direction of arrows flashing on a computer screen for way too long.

A bit like working on an assembly line day after day, until pushing the wrong button becomes inevitable. Or attending an endless office meeting where you stopped paying attention altogether—until, that is, you're called upon unexpectedly and blurt out the wrong answer.

ANSWERS

THE SENIOR MOMENTS MAGIC SQUARE *page 11*

ZERO	NIL	0
NOUGHT	NULL	VOID
ZIP	NADA	NOTHING

ON BEYOND *ROSEBUD* *page 12*
1—c, 2—d, 3—b, 4—a

AH, TO BE YOUNGER . . . *page 13*
The trick is in the dates. If the year 1206 is actually 1206 BC (or BCE),
it came five years *before*, not after, 1201.

HOME SWEET HOME *page 13*
The masked man is the catcher of the opposing team. Bob is playing baseball.

"REMEMBER ME," SAID TOM MEMORABLY *pages 14-15*
Here are my favorite answers (although yours may be just as good or
better): 1—thoughtlessly, 2—rabidly, 3—professed, 4—icily, 5—doggedly,
6—conviction, 7—abstractly, 8—admitted, 9—chimed in, 10—darkly,
11—nagged, 12—chirped, 13—thundered, 14—gagged, 15—sourly

BEGINNINGS AND ENDINGS *page 16*
T, R, and E are the first three new letters and I, N, and G are the second three,
which gives you TREKKING and TREATING.

BRAINY BOTTLENECK *page 17*
Just push the cork into the bottle and shake the coin out.

BRAIN is to BODY as _____ is to BOAT *pages 18-19*
1—b, 2—c, 3—b, 4—c, 5—a, 6—c, 7—b, 8—c, 9—b

A FLAGGING MEMORY *pages 21-22*
B

THE MONTY HALL BRAINTEASER *page 23*
Intuitively, you would think that your odds of getting the car are fifty-fifty. After all, there are still two doors closed, and either one might have the car, right? Well, as it turns out, you should switch. When you stick with Door Number One, you win only if your original choice was correct. But that only happens one in three times. Why? Because you started with three doors, not two doors. However—and here is where it gets a bit mind-bending—if you switch to Door Number Three, you win if your original choice was wrong, which happens two out of three times. Again, remember that you had to pick among three doors originally, and two out of three have a goat behind it. So you should switch to Door Number Three. (If you don't believe me, play the game yourself, as game theorists, probability experts, the *New York Times*, and Monty Hall suggest.)

COMMON WORDS IN COMMON *page 26*
The letter *R* moves one place in each consecutive word, from first (**R**ESTAURANT) to seventh (LACQUE**R**) back to first (**R**ELEASED, and then the second letter (A**R**TIFICIAL) and ending as the third letter (PA**R**TICLE).

THINK INSIDE THE BOX *page 29*
Four "gives" and four "gets," or "forgives and forgets"

COLOR THIS PUZZLE   *page 29*

Ms. Gray wore green, Ms. White wore gray, and Ms. Green wore white. Here's why: Since no one was wearing the same color as her name, Ms. Gray had to be wearing either green or white. But since the woman who agreed with her was already wearing white, Ms. Gray must have been wearing green. Ms. White, on the other hand, could only have been wearing gray or green, and since we already know that Ms. Gray was wearing green, Ms. White must have been wearing gray. That leaves the woman who was wearing white, who could only have been Ms. Green, the last of the three.

BRAIN POWER PUSH-UPS   *pages 31-32*
1—b, 2—c, 3—b

WHERE WERE YOU IN THE FIFTIES?   *page 33*
1—d, 2—c, 3—e, 4—b, 5—a

BRAINY WORD SEARCH   *page 35*

O	D	U	M	C	E	M	**S**	P	U	H	C
E	R	M	E	A	U	**Y**	Y	L	G	R	N
M	**M**	**A**	O	S	**N**	U	E	H	E	R	D
S	**U**	**P**	**M**	**A**	**C**	**O**	**P**	**P**	**I**	**H**	O
R	**L**	**R**	**P**	Y	U	H	X	C	N	H	R
N	**L**	**S**	**B**	D	**G**	Y	L	P	R	G	O
E	**E**	**E**	**E**	**C**	**D**	S	S	R	C	R	
M	**B**	U	**P**	**O**	**R**	**R**	**A**	M	S	N	M
M	**E**	R	**R**	G	M	**E**	M	**L**	C	B	S
M	**R**	T	U	O	X	B	**C**	P	**A**	B	R
S	**E**	O	L	A	**N**	R	E	E	L	O	S
X	**C**	Y	R	E	U	R	R	A	S	N	R

{117}

TAKE THAT! *page 40*
"I said that, 'that "that" that that man wrote should have been underlined.'"

SUITS YOU TO A *T* *page 40*
True. There are just two *uppercase T*'s.

YESTERDAY . . . *page 43*
1—c, 2—a, 3—d, 4—b

DOUBLE OR NOTHING *page 45*
Coming after 2,048 are: 4,096, 8,192, 16,384, 32,768, 65,536, 131,072, 262,144, 524,288, and 1,048,576.

ROW YOUR BOAT ASHORE *page 46*
First, the twins paddle to the opposite side of the river while Michael stays put. Then Jane gets out while Jim heads back across. When Jim reaches Michael, Jim gets out and his father gets in. Then Michael paddles across the river, leaving Jim behind. When Michael reaches the other side, he gets out, and Jane gets in and goes back for Jim. Finally, the twins paddle across the river together to join their father.

TRACKING YOUR PROGRESS *page 49*
Second place. Why? If you overtake the person in second place, that means you were in third place. And the person who was in first place is still in front of you.

WORDS IN HIDING *pages 50-51*
1—horse (I ab**hor se**ntimentality and pretence!)
2—salad (Mary passe**s a lad**le for the pea soup.)
3—gun (He will be walkin**g un**less he is riding.)
4—ankle (The new t**ank le**d the squad into battle.)

5—Paris (Gas**par is** a fine young man.)

6—dress (The Chinese ca**dres s**ang patriotic songs.)

7—Everest (He n**ever est**imates if he can be exact.)

8—tabletop (He was no**t able to p**aint yesterday.)

9—pine (Don't ste**p in e**lephant dung!)

10—halo (Cas**h a lo**cal check at a local bank.)

11—shaker (A smart person don't **shake r**attle snakes.)

12—pinch (What do you do if she won't s**pin ch**ickens?)

13—heart (T**he art**s are badly funded these days.)

14—escargot (His fak**e scar got** torn off.)

15—slightly (She sell**s light ly**res on the seashore.)

"YOU WERE THERE" . . . *page 53*

1—b, 2—a, 3—d, 4—c

MOTHER GOOSE'S REVENGE *page 54*

Since the narrator is going to St. Ives, those other folks (and kits, cats, and sacks) that he met on the road are coming *from* St. Ives. So the answer is one—the narrator.

THE CIRCLE GAME *page 56*

Move the O at the top right of the first row and the O in the middle of the bottom row in Illustration One to the position of the bottom two O's in Illustration Two.

GOING UP? *page 57*

John is only ten years old and short for his age, so he cannot reach the elevator buttons for the upper floors. He can, however, ask someone else to push the button for the 10th floor. Or, if he has an umbrella (that's where the rain comes in), he can push the button himself. Otherwise, he can only reach the button for the 7th floor, get off there, and walk up the rest of the way.

THE RAIN IN SPAIN . . . *page 60*
1—e, 2—a, 3—d, 4—c, 5—b

FROM LETTERS TO WORDS *page 61*
1—*LIE*, 2—*LIVE*, 3—*LIVER*, 4—*DRIVEL*, 5—*RIVALED*

REALER THAN REAL . . . *page 63*
1—d, 2—e, 3—a, 4—b, 5—c
Bonus Answer: Atlantis the Capital

***T* IS FOR THINK FAST** *page 65*
Tabasco, tablet, tackle, tankard, tattle, Teflon, tempest, teriyaki, tinsel, tirade, toddler, tomahawk, trampoline, trolley, troubadour, tundra, tick tock, troll, toll, telephone

SENIOR MOMENTS REBUS *page 66*
"forgetful" (i.e., full of forgets)

RETURN TO WOODSTOCK *page 68*
Joni Mitchell, The Byrds, Bob Dylan, and Eric Clapton
Bonus answers:
1. Richie Havens opened the festival with "High Flyin' Bird."
2. Joni Mitchell wrote and performed the song "Woodstock," even though she wasn't there.
3. Crosby, Stills, Nash & Young made it a hit.

FROM HERE TO THERE *pages 70-71*
The rule is as follows: Each colored square, gray or black, moves to the right (or to the beginning of the next row) and then changes to the opposite color.

So FIGURE C should be

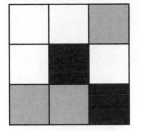

REMEMBER THAT TRIP TO WHEREVER? *page 72*
1, 3, and 4 are the same length (5,383 miles). number 2, however, is far longer and would require an amphibious car. (On the other hand, you could make a side trip to Paris.)

JOIN THE GROUP *page 74*
Japan, Australia, and Madagascar are island nations.
Switzerland, Syria, and Mexico are not.

ENDINGS AND BEGINNINGS *page 75*
BLU are the first three letters and **ERS** are the last three, for BLU**ND**ERS and BLU**ST**ERS.

WHO SAID IT? *pages 77-78*
1—a, 2—c, 3—c, 4—a, 5—b, 6—c, 7—b

DOUBLE YOUR FUN *page 81*

L	I	N	T
I	D	E	A
N	E	C	K
T	A	K	E

TEN-SECOND DASH   *page 83*
1—8, 2—14, 3—11

NINE DOTS TO A SHARPER BRAIN   *page 84*

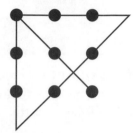

(Start from the dot in the lower right corner.)

A HARD WORD TO REMEMBER   *pages 85-86*
3—athazagoraphobia

UNRULY LETTERS   *pages 87-88*
1—d (lilac), 2—b (milliliter), 3—c (nemesis), 4—a (roulette),
5—c (vampire), 6—b (Algiers), 7—d (*War and Peace*)

YOU WERE THERE   *page 89*
1—b, 2—a, 3—d, 4—c

THE TREASURE OR THE TIGER   *page 91*
Ask either one what the other would say if asked which door has the treasure
behind it. Then you open the other door. Why? If you ask the knight, he will
answer truthfully that the other man (the thief) will lie and claim that the
knight will say that the door with the tiger has the treasure behind it. On the
other hand, if you ask the thief, he will lie and say that the knight will tell you
to open the door with the tiger. So either way, you should always open the
other door.

A RISING TIDE *page 92*
No rungs, in either case. A rising tide lifts both the boat *and* the rope ladder.

CRACK THE CODE *page 92*
These are all lines from *Hamlet*, written backwards.
1. Neither a borrower nor a lender be
2. Brevity is the soul of wit
3. O that this too, too solid flesh would melt
4. We know what we are, but know not what we may be

RIDDLE YOU THIS *pages 94-95*
1—a coat of paint, 2—a cold, 3—the word *wholesome*, 4—a river,
5—a stamp, 6—breath, 7—footsteps, 8—the sun, 9—your word,
10—your name, 11—silence, 12—noise, 13—a deck of cards,
14—a sponge, 15—a riddle

SCRABBLE SCRAMBLE *page 96*
FORGETS

NAME THAT GURU! *page 98*
1—b, 2—c, 3—d, 4—a
Bonus Answer: After "Hare Krishna Hare Krishna" comes "Krishna Krishna
Hare Hare, Hare Rama Hare Rama, Rama Rama Hare Hare."

RACING HORSES *page 99*
He told them to switch horses. That way, whoever won the race would be
riding his/her sibling's horse, which would then make it the faster one, and
thus the loser. At the same time, their own horse would be the slower of the
two, and thus the real winner according to the father's rules.

HAVE A BALL! *page 102*
Just throw the ball straight up in the air.

. . . A LONG WEEK *page 102*
Tuesday, Thursday, today, and tomorrow

DOT YOUR *I*'S *page 103*
There are 24 *i*'s.

WHAT COMES NEXT? *page 104*
1. January, December, November, October, **S**(eptember), **A**(ugust),
   J(uly), **J**(une)
2. Three, Four, Five, Six, **S**(even), **E**(ight), **N**(ine), **T**(en)
3. Hoover, Roosevelt, Truman, Eisenhower, **K**(ennedy), **J**(ohnson),
   N(ixon), **F**(ord)

WORDS, WORDS, WORDS *page 106*
1—slow, 2—hard, 3—stop, 4—life, 5—show, 6—cheese, 7—hand,
8—box, 9—eye, 10—wood, 11—spot

YOU WERE THERE *page 107*
1—b, 2—d, 3—a, 4—c

TIPPING THE SCALES OF FORTUNE *page 109*
You need to weigh the coins three times. **(1)** Divide the 24 coins into three
groups of eight coins each. If the first two groups you put on the scale weigh
the same, then you know the heavier coin isn't in either one and must be
in the third group. If one of the first two groups is heavier than the other,
however, you know the rare coin must be in that group. **(2)** Take the group
with thc heavier coin and break it up into three smaller groups: one with
three coins, the second with three coins, and the third with two coins. Now

weigh the two groups of three coins to find out if one is heavier than the other. If so, set the heavier group aside. If not, the heavier coin must be in the group with two coins. **(3)** If one of the groups with three coins is heavier, weigh two of the coins against each other. If a coin tips the scales, then that's the rare coin. If the first two coins weigh the same, however, then the other, third coin must be the one you want. On the other hand, if it's the group of two coins that has the heavier coin, simply weigh each of the two against the other to find the right one.

In any case, you only need to weigh the coins three times.

AND THE NEXT NUMBER IS . . . *page 110*
1—c (4+3=7, +5=12, +7=19, +9=28, +11=39)
2—a (6+14=20, + 7=27, +14=41, +7=48, +14=62)
3—c (23-7=16, -6=10, -5=5, -4=1, -3=-2
4—b (9x2=18, x3=54, x4=216, x5=1,080, x6=6,480)

THE MISSING LINKS *pages 112-113*
The vowels are missing from familiar sections of two great historical documents.

1. The Preamble of the Declaration of Independence:
"We hold these truths to be self-evident, that all men are created equal, that they are endowed by their Creator with certain unalienable Rights, that among these are Life, Liberty, and the pursuit of Happiness. That to secure these rights, Governments are instituted among Men, deriving their just powers from the consent of the governed. That whenever any Form of Government becomes destructive of these ends, it is the Right of the People to alter or to abolish it, and to institute new Government, laying its foundation on such principles and organizing its powers in such form, as to them shall seem most likely to effect their Safety and Happiness."

2. The end of the Gettysburg Address:
"The world will little note, nor long remember what we say here, but it can never forget what they did here. It is for us the living, rather, to be dedicated here to the unfinished work which they who fought here have thus far so nobly advanced. It is rather for us to be here dedicated to the great task remaining before us—that from these honored dead we take increased devotion to that cause for which they gave the last full measure of devotion—that we here highly resolve that these dead shall not have died in vain—that this nation, under God, shall have a new birth of freedom—and that government of the people, by the people, for the people, shall not perish from the earth."

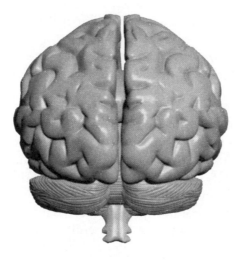

ACKNOWLEDGMENTS

I'll try to keep these really short so as not to strain my memory or yours.

First, my sincerest thanks to Richard Rosen, who made possible my first foray into humor, *1,000 Unforgettable Senior Moments*, and then volunteered to read the early drafts of this book. Clearly, some people are just gluttons for punishment and compulsively generous.

Let me also thank my editor at Sterling Publishing, Katherine Furman, who did such a superlative job. May she rise to the very top of the publishing world (and throw a few absurdly lucrative book deals my way).

Additional thanks to designers Michael Rogalski and Melissa Gerber. If the book does well, it will be due in no small part to their inspired work.

Next, a round of fervent applause to Paul Bresnick, my indefatigable, blessedly accomplished agent. (May he actually get me those future, absurdly lucrative book deals.)

Finally, everything inevitably leads back to Christy, whose support, incredible stamina (how may drafts were there, anyway?), and inexplicable love makes it all possible.

ABOUT THE AUTHOR

Tom Friedman is the author of the best-selling book *1,000 Unforgettable Senior Moments* Of Which We Could Remember Only 246* (Workman Publishing, 2006). A writer, editor, and documentary producer, he worked in public television for nearly 25 years, at its flagship station, WGBH Boston. In 1996, he won a George Foster Peabody Award—the Pulitzer Prize of broadcasting—for the critically acclaimed science documentary series, *Odyssey of Life*. He is also the author of two books about business and economics: *Life and Death on the Corporate Battlefield*, with Paul Solman, and *Up the Ladder*. He lives in California.

{ "THEY MAY FORGET WHAT YOU SAID, BUT THEY WILL NEVER FORGET HOW YOU MADE THEM FEEL." }

—Carl W. Buechner